AF488451

SAID THE
TIGER

TO THE
RABBIT

SAID THE TIGER

TO THE RABBIT

A book of haiku texts and expressionistic paintings from

SR. SHARIFA VERNICE MEYTUNG-MA

Published by Sr. Sharifa Vernice Meytung-Ma

Hardback ISBN: 979-8-218-49106-2

Cover design by Oskar Castro, Bohiti Fotuto Productions
Book interior design by Curtis Key
Back cover photo credit: Naomi Ishisaka

This book is dedicated to Clarissa Rogers (November 12, 1967 - March 17, 2024). An urban bodhisattva and working-class theorist whose spiritual journey I was blessed to accompany for part of the way . . . Let the wacky adventures continue!

"In order to have a society where workers manage themselves collectively, we need all of our best group process skills. To have a culture that values all voices and all people equally in decision-making, we need to practice ways of working together that don't reproduce oppression. Deliberation takes practice!"

-Clarissa Rogers

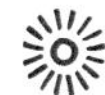

Dieses Buch ist Clarissa Rogers (12. November 1967 – 17. März 2024) gewidmet. Ein urbaner Bodhisattva und Theoretikerin der Arbeiterklasse, deren spirituelle Reise, ich das Glück hatte, einen Teil des Weges zu begleiten . . . Lass die verrückten Abenteuer fortsetzen!

„Um eine Gesellschaft zu schaffen, in der Arbeitnehmer sich kollektiv verwalten, brauchen wir all unsere besten Fähigkeiten im Bereich der Gruppenprozesse. In einer Kultur, die alle Stimmen und alle Menschen bei der Entscheidungsfindung gleichermaßen wertschätzt, müssen wir Formen der Zusammenarbeit praktizieren, die keine Unterdrückung reproduziert. Bedacht braucht Übung!"

-Clarissa Rogers

Ein paar Worte der Autorin…

Seit dem 13. Jahrhundert n. Chr. gibt die Kalachakra Version des tibetischen Kalenders jedem neuen Jahr Tiernamen. Die Namen werden in 60-Jahres-Zyklen rotiert. Die ausgewählten Tiere sind Hase, Drache, Schlange, Pferd, Schaf, Affe, Vogel, Hund, Wildschwein, Ratte, Ochse und Tiger, in dieser Reihenfolge. 2023 war das Jahr des Wasserhasen (auch bekannt als Wasserkaninchen). Das vorangegangene Jahr war das Jahr des Wassertigers. Dieses Jahr, 2024, ist das Jahr des Walddrachen.

Ich bin dieses Wochenende in New York City und nehme an einem Zazen-Meditationsretreat teil. Es ist das Wochenende vor meinem 65. Geburtstag, der am Dienstag, dem 12. März, ansteht. Als ich am Freitagabend in meinem Hotel ankam, stellte ich fest, dass der Herd in der Küchenzeile defekt war. Zum Glück wurde ich in ein neues Zimmer verlegt, was ich sehr schätzte, da ich auf Reisen alles selbst koche. Die neue Zimmernummer war 1212 … das zwölfte Zimmer im zwölften Stock. Da mein Geburtstag am zwölften März ist, habe ich diese Geste und Anspielung aus der Welt der Zahlen und Symbole sehr geschätzt. Und das sind für mich die Kalenderjahr-Tiernamen. Es sind Symbole, die auf Potenzial hinweisen.

Mögest du das Potenzial jedes dieser kurzen Gedichte in diesem Buch erkunden. Jedes Gedicht hat nur siebzehn Silben (mit Ausnahme von Nr. 29), um dir eine Welt zu zeigen, die … innerhalb eines Augenblicks sein könnte. Jedes Haiku ist auf Englisch verfasst und ins Deutsche übersetzt. Dies ist eine Anspielung auf die über fünfzehn Jahre, die ich in West- und Ostdeutschland gelebt, geschrieben, geführt, gespielt, studiert, unterrichtet und meine Kinder großgezogen habe. Ich schulde Karoline Malik großen Dank für ihre großzügige, herzhafte Übersetzung meiner Worte und Gedanken in die deutsche Sprache.

Neben der Poesie, mögen auch jedes der ausdrucksstarken Gemälde zu dir sprechen, vom Potenzial, vollkommen im Moment unseres Lebens präsent zu sein. „Sei ganz präsent", hat der Wassertiger meiner Meinung nach dem Wasserkaninchen ins Ohr geflüstert, und das wünsche ich dir, lieber Leser . . . möge es so sein.

Sr. Sharifa Vernice Meytung-Ma
New York, New York
11. März 2024

A few words from the author...

Since the 13th century C.E., the Kalachakra version of the Tibetan calendar has given animal names to each new year. The names are rotated through sixty-year cycles. The chosen animals are the hare, dragon, snake, horse, sheep, monkey, bird, dog, boar, rat, ox, and tiger, in that order. 2023 was the Year of the Water Hare (aka Water Rabbit). The preceding year was the Year of the Water Tiger; 2024 is the Year of the Wood Dragon.

I am in New York City this weekend, participating in a Zazen meditation retreat. It's the weekend before my 65th birthday, which comes up on Tuesday, March 12th. When I arrived at my hotel on Friday evening, I discovered that the kitchenette had a defective stove. Thankfully, I was moved to a new room which I appreciated, as I do all of my own cooking when I travel. The new room number was 1212 . . . the twelfth room, on the twelfth floor. Given that my birthday is on the twelfth of March, I appreciated this nod and wink from the world of numbers and symbols. And that's what the calendar year animal names are for me. They are symbols that point to potential.

May you explore the potential of each of these short poems in this book. Each poem has only seventeen syllables (with the exception of #29) to show you a world that could be . . . within a moment that is. Each haiku is written in English and translated into German. This is a nod to the over fifteen years I spent living, writing, guiding, performing, studying, teaching and raising my children in both West and East Germany. I owe a debt of gratitude to Karoline Malik for her generous heart-translation of my words and thoughts into the German language.

In addition to the poetry, may each of the expressive paintings speak to you of the potential of being fully present to each moment of our lives. Be fully present, is what I think the Water tiger whispered into the ear of the Water Rabbit, and is what I wish for you, dear reader . . . May It Be So.

Sr. Sharifa Vernice Meytung-Ma
New York, New York
March 11, 2024

HAIKU

Ein Haiku ist eine ungereimte japanische Gedichtform, die aus 17 Silben besteht, die in drei Zeilen mit jeweils fünf, sieben und fünf Silben angeordnet sind. Ein Haiku drückt in möglichst wenigen Worten viel aus und suggeriert mehr.

EXPRESSIONISTISCHE MALEREI

Der Expressionismus ist eine Theorie oder Praxis in der Kunst, die versucht, subjektive Emotionen und Reaktionen darzustellen, die Objekte und Ereignisse beim Künstler hervorrufen.

A Few Helpful Definitions (courtesy of the Merriam Webster dictionary) . . .

HAIKU

A haiku is an unrhymed Japanese poetic form that consists of 17 syllables arranged in three lines containing five, seven, and five syllables, respectively. A haiku expresses much and suggests more in the fewest possible words.

EXPRESSIONISTIC PAINTING

Expressionism is a theory or practice in art of seeking to depict the subjective emotions and responses that objects and events arouse in the artist.

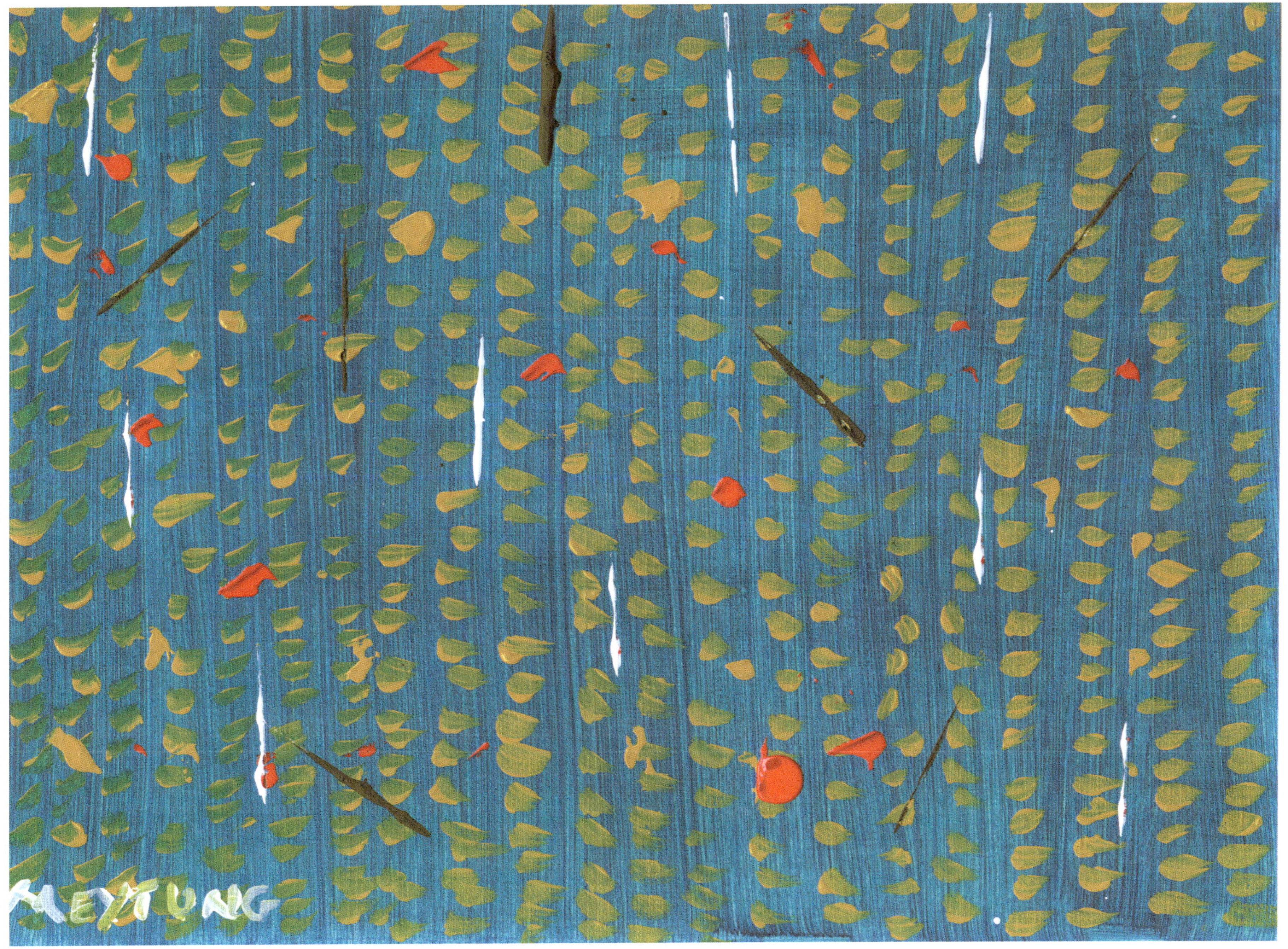

Teaming with Life

ART RESIDENCY HAIKU

residency ends
as the final colors dry
new ideas arise

das Künstler-Retreat endet
während die letzten Farben trocknen
entstehen neue Ideen

LIBERTINY'S HONEY-VASE

artists and bees swarm
as the scaffolding disappears
a honey-vase forms . . .

Künstler und Bienen schwärmen
als das Gerüst schwindet
entsteht eine Honigvase

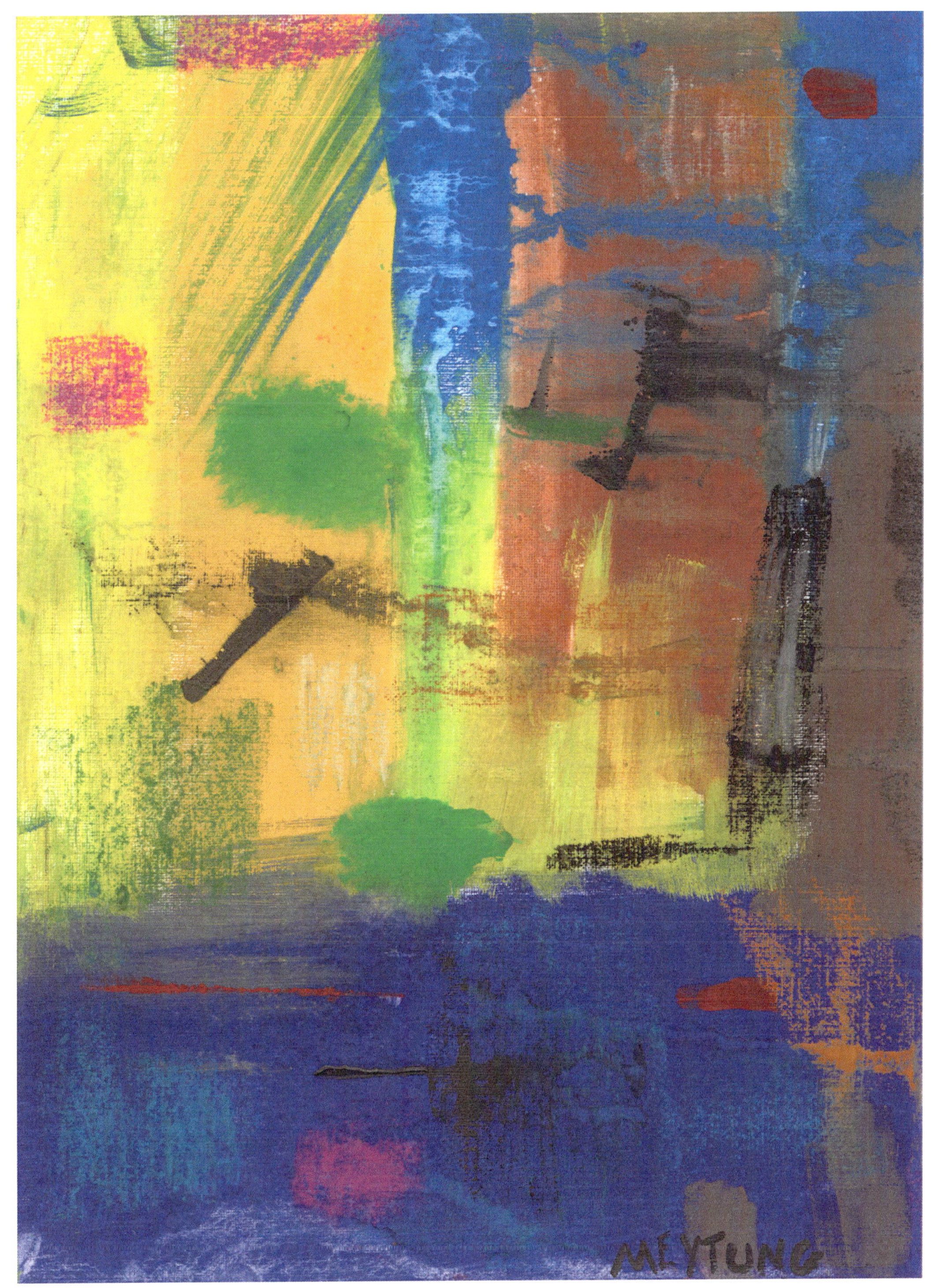

FOR GEORGE

from Jerusalem
through to Minneapolis
Mamas bear witness

aus Jerusalem
bis nach Minneapolis
Mütter legen Zeugnis ab

Retrieved

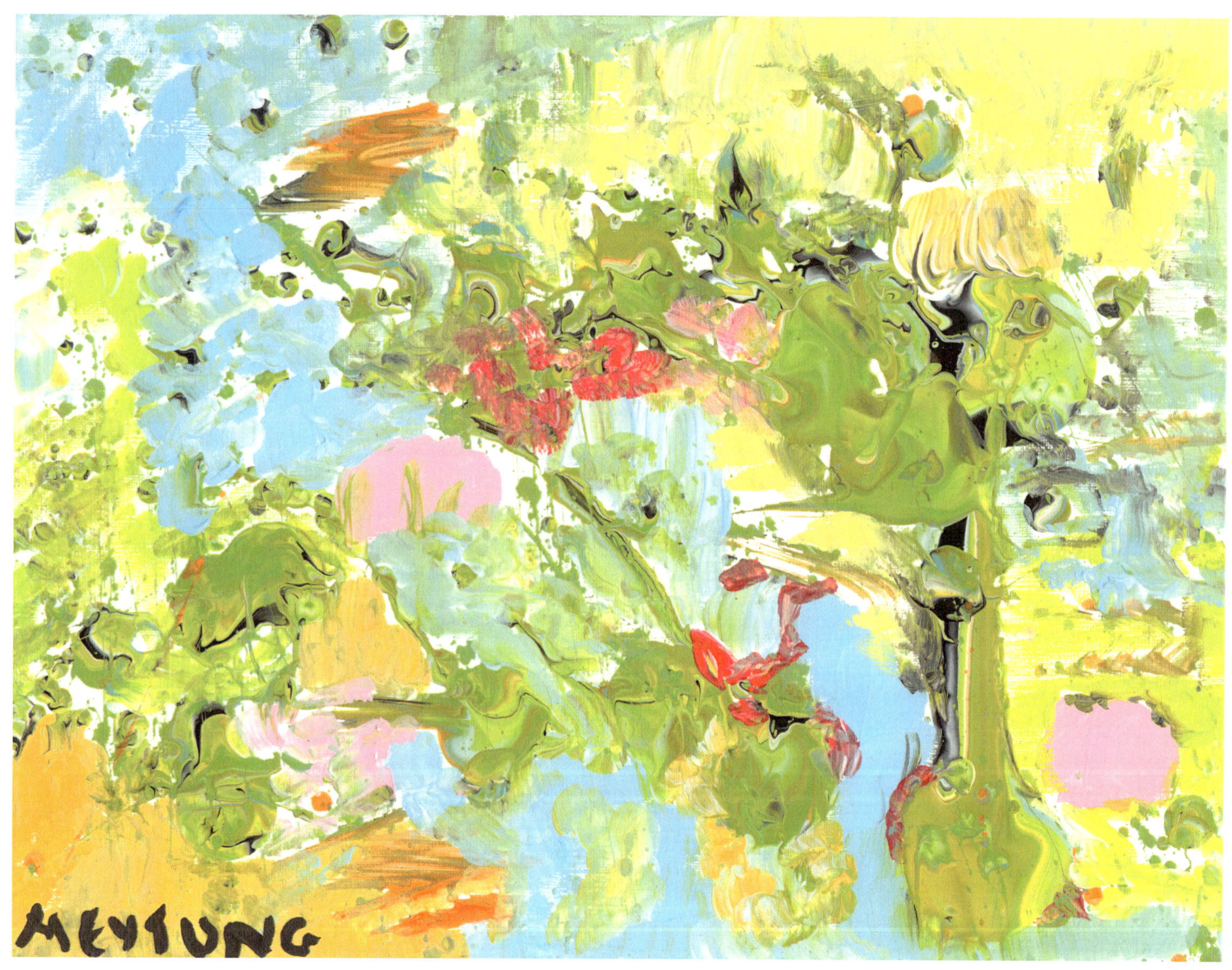

Here In Bartram's Garden

THE CROSSING

deer mother and child
mother makes it while child
waits
our truck rambles on

die Hirschmutter und ihr Kind
die Mutter schafft es, während
das Kind wartet
unser Wagen zieht weiter

SEARCH

covered in moisture
green valley in summer mist
trees lush and dripping

mit Feuchtigkeit bedeckt
das grüne Tal im Sommernebel
Bäume üppig bewachsen und tropfend nass

GRID

living in the grid
where power never fails us
re-generation

das Leben im Stromnetz
wo uns die Macht nie verfehlt
Erneuerung

TO INCARNATE

manifestation
and "re-manifestation"
Buddha's vijñapti

Erscheinung
und Wiedererscheinung
Buddhas Vijñapti

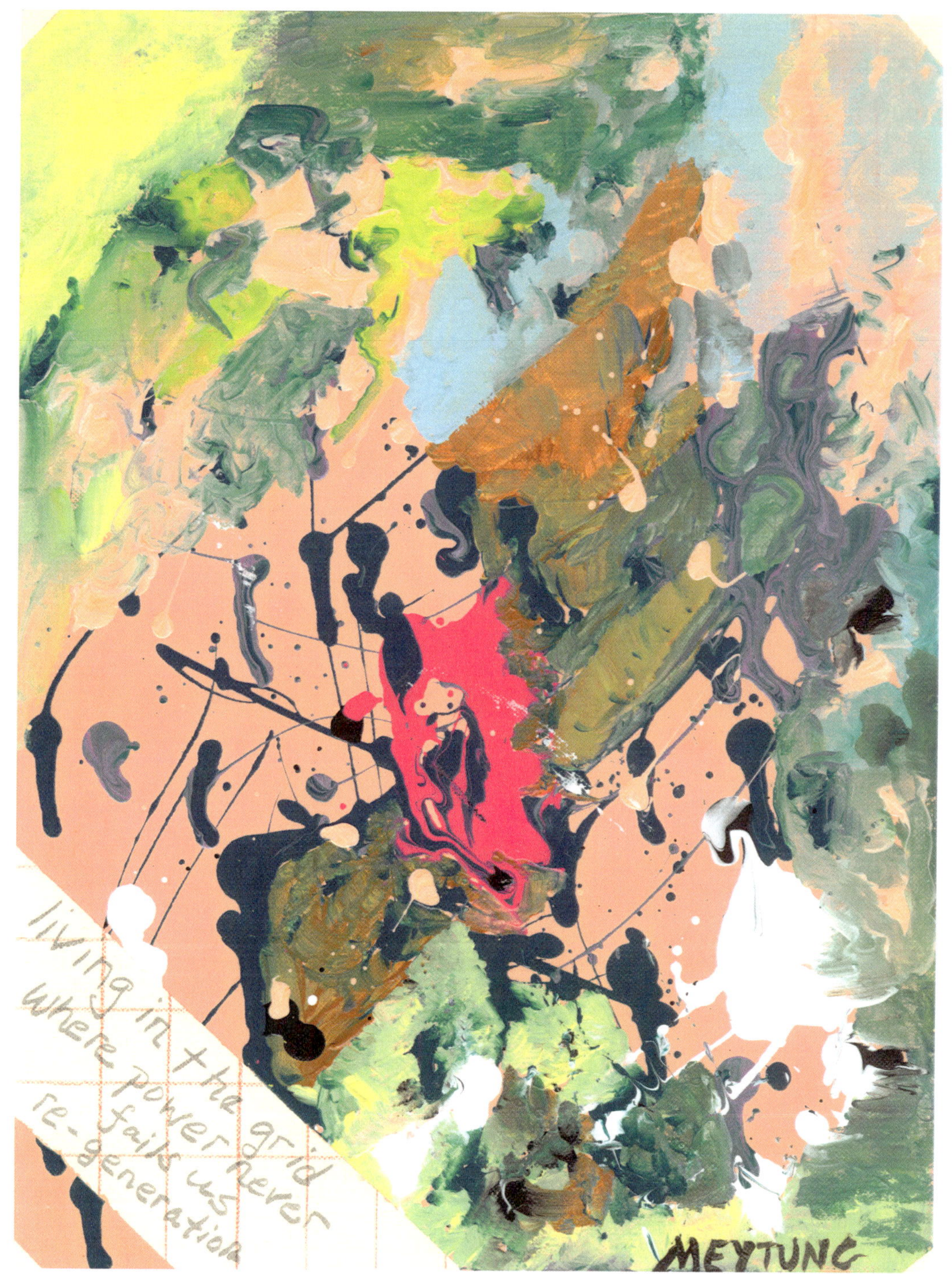

Grid

JP

dancing in stillness
like Pollock before me
there's peace in this paint

Tanzen in der Stille
wie Pollock vor mir
in der Farbe ist Frieden

KOAN #1

what are you doing?
echoes heard in consciousness
as memory fades

Was machst du?
Echos, hörbar im Bewusstsein
während die Erinnerung verblass

FOR TUPAC

bits of broken glass
lay shattered on the concrete
will the rose still grow?

Glasscherben
lagen verstreut auf dem Beton
wird die Rose noch wachsen?

FOR RAHIM THE FOUNDER

E.G.O.* shook the ground
Hiphop sprouted from quaked earth
we who were there, know

E.G.O.* erschütterte den Boden
HipHop sprießt aus bebender Erde
Wir, die dabei waren, wissen Bescheid

*Author's Note: E.G.O. - Erfurter Ground Organization was a seminal youth-led initiative promoting the elements of Hiphop Culture. It was founded in the 1990's by Hiphop artists/entrepreneurs Abdul Rahim Malik & "Manu" in Erfurt, Germany.

*Anmerkung des Autors: E.G.O. - Erfurter Ground Organization war eine grundlegende Jugendinitiative zur Förderung der Hip-Hop-Kultur und deren Elemente. Diese wurde in den 1990er Jahren vom Hip-Hop-Künstler/Unternehmer Abdul Rahim Malik & "Manu" in Erfurt, Deutschland gegründet.

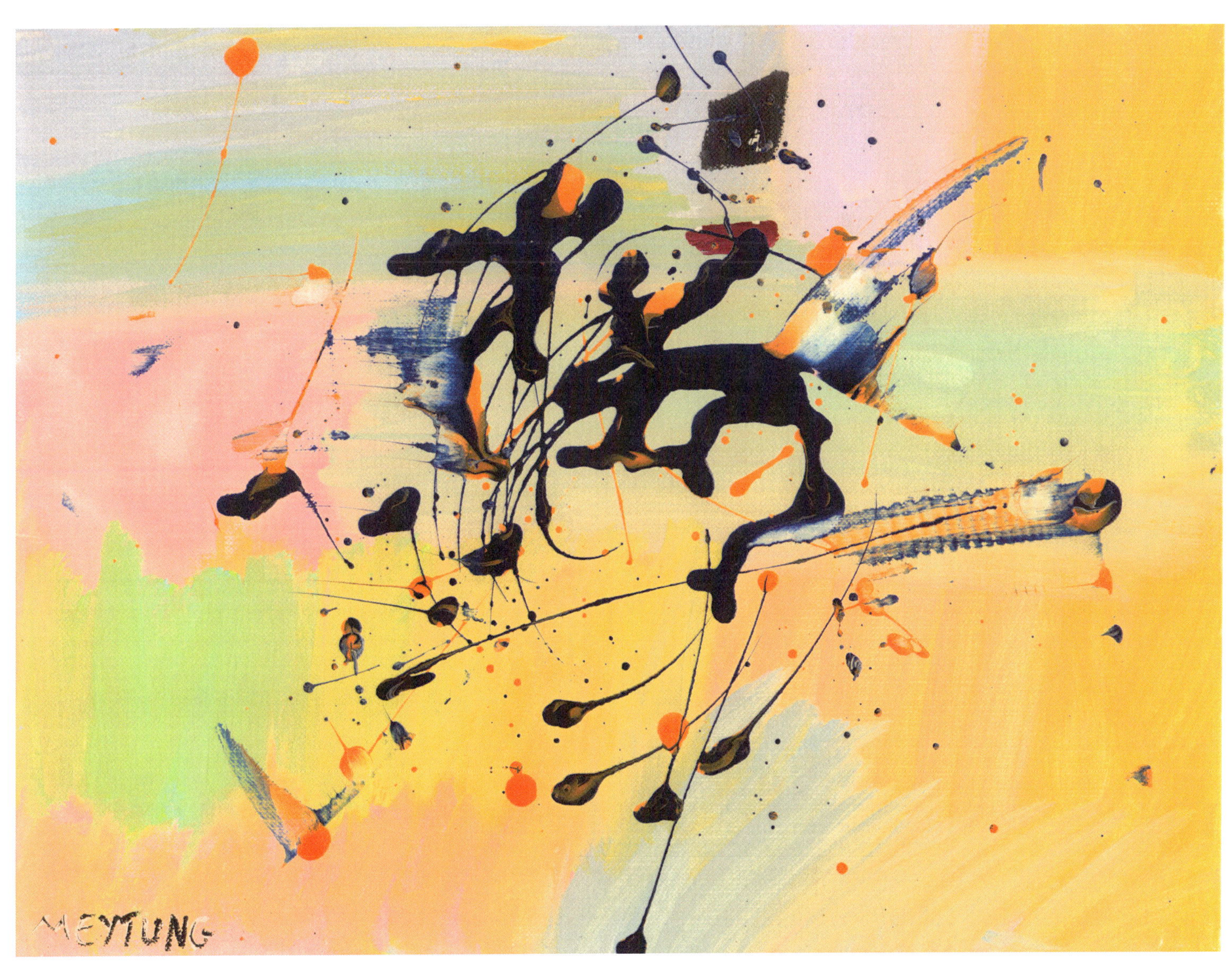

Dancing Dolphins

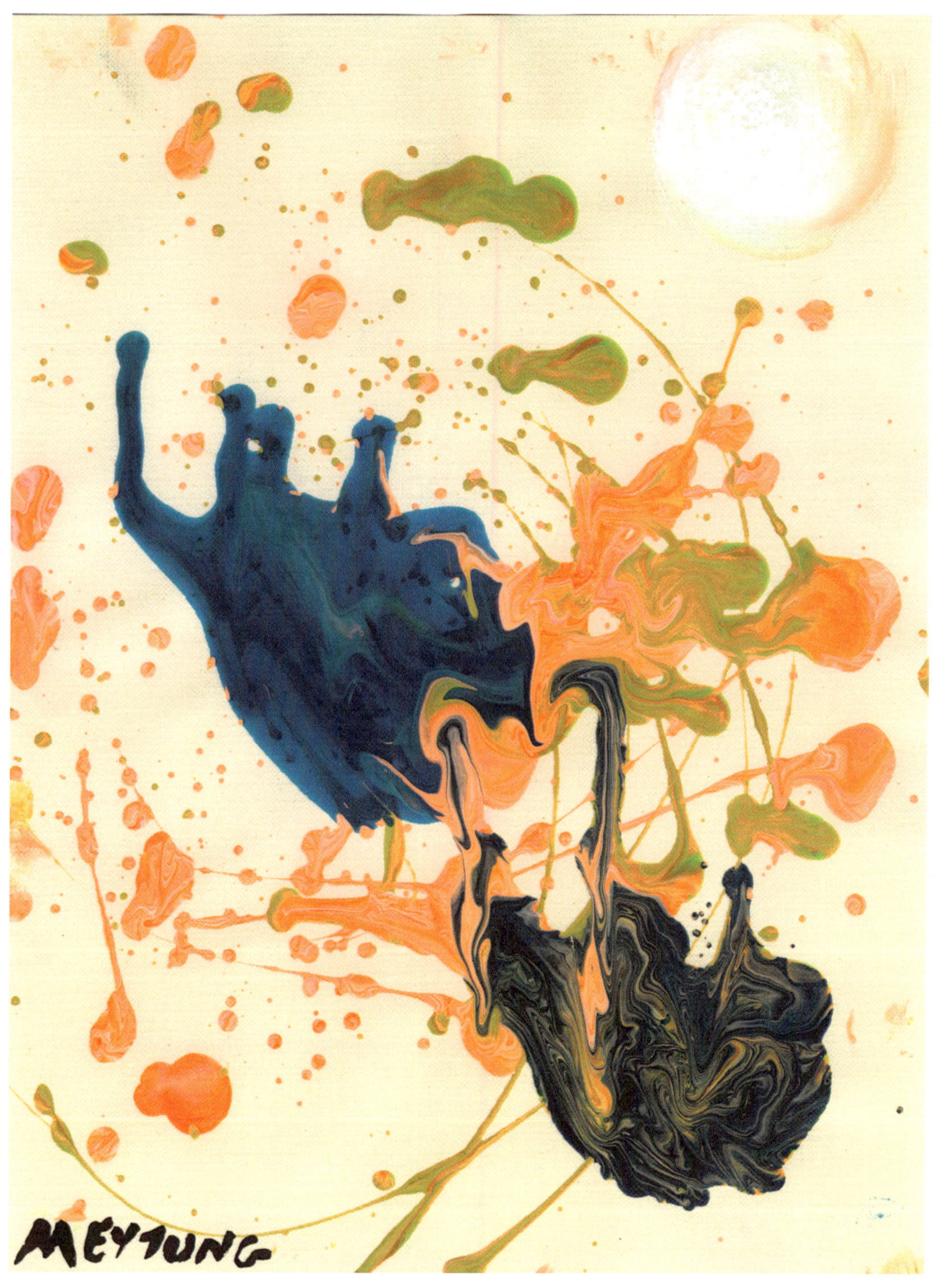

ALL HALLOW'S EVE

out of the cauldron
leaping into the moonlight
a Halloween dance

aus dem Kessel
hervorspringend aus dem
Mondlicht
ein Halloween-Tanz

Out of the Cauldron and into the Moonlight

HAIL MARY

What had happened was . . .
Henry Ossawa Tanner's
"Annunciation"

Was passiert ist, war . . .
Henry Ossawa Tanners
"Verkündigung"

LIBRARY BLUES

histories untold
Lead Belly sings, "best stay
woke"
truth on dusty shelves

verschwiegende Geschichte
Lead Belly singt, "bleib am
besten wachsam"
die Wahrheit auf staubigen
Regalen

THE CHAIR

sliver of sunlight
as gentle as a friend's smile
invites me to sit

Sonnenstrahl
so sanft wie das Lächeln eines
Freundes
lädt mich zum Sitzen ein

ON MY WAY TO WORK

bee sting on trolley
train barrels towards newness
last stop for the bee

Bienenstich in der Straßenbahn
die Bahn brettert neuen Gelegenheiten entgegen
letzter Halt für die Biene

PARK SIGHTING

here, amongst concrete
a black squirrel has crossed my path
i doubted my eyes

hier, zwischen Beton
ist mir ein schwarzes Eichhörnchen
über den Weg gelaufen
ich traute meinen Augen nicht

Primordial Movement

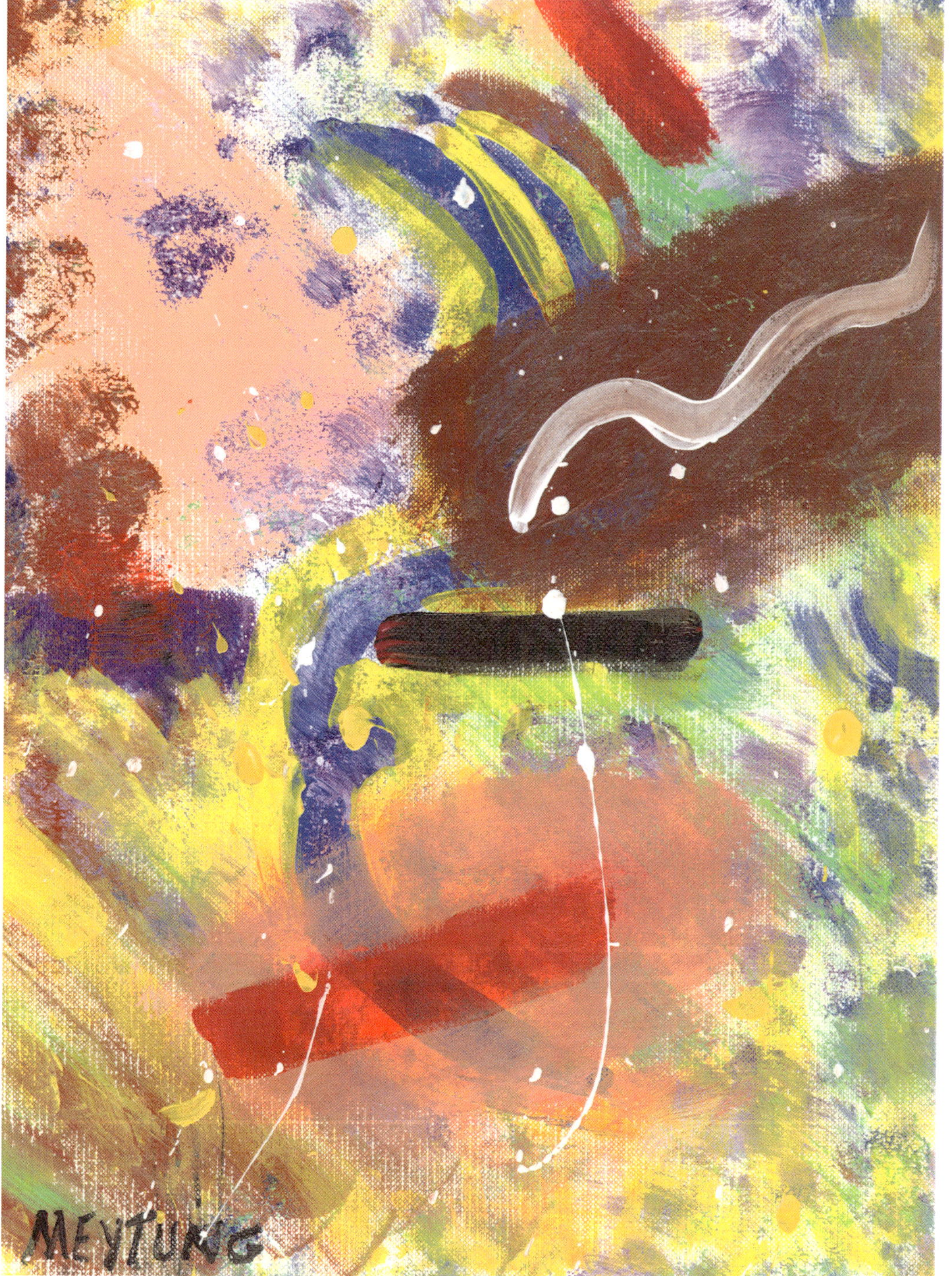

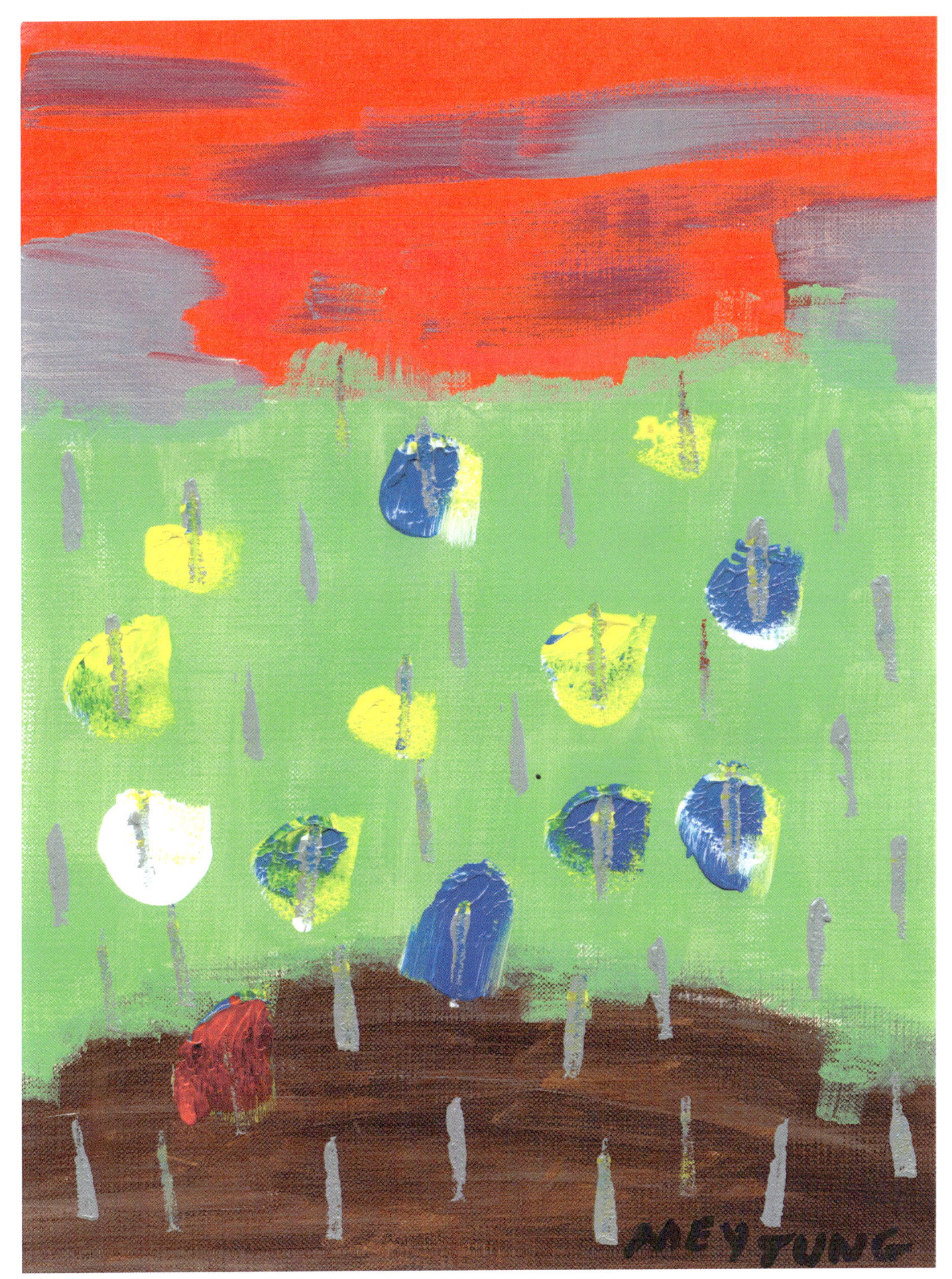

INTERPERMEATED

floating Milky Way
billion-light-years-wide bubble
impermanent home

schwebende Milchstraße
eine Milliarden Lichtjahre breite
Blase
unbeständiges Zuhause

Is It Really Grey When It Rains

LOOKING OUT

heat streams through window
panes stretch from ceiling to floor
rippling waves of sun

Wärme strömt durch das Fenster
Fensterscheiben strecken sich von der
Decke bis zum Boden
kräuselnde Wellen der Sonne

FOR JAN O.

where does sound begin
and do we know where it ends
when there are no words . . .

Wo beginnt ein Klang
und wissen wir, wo er endet
wenn es keine Worte gibt . . .

WHO'S IN THE MOON

the Full Moon reveals
smiles in surprising places
and that is enough . . .

der Vollmond enthüllt
Lächeln an überraschenden
Stellen
und das ist genug . . .

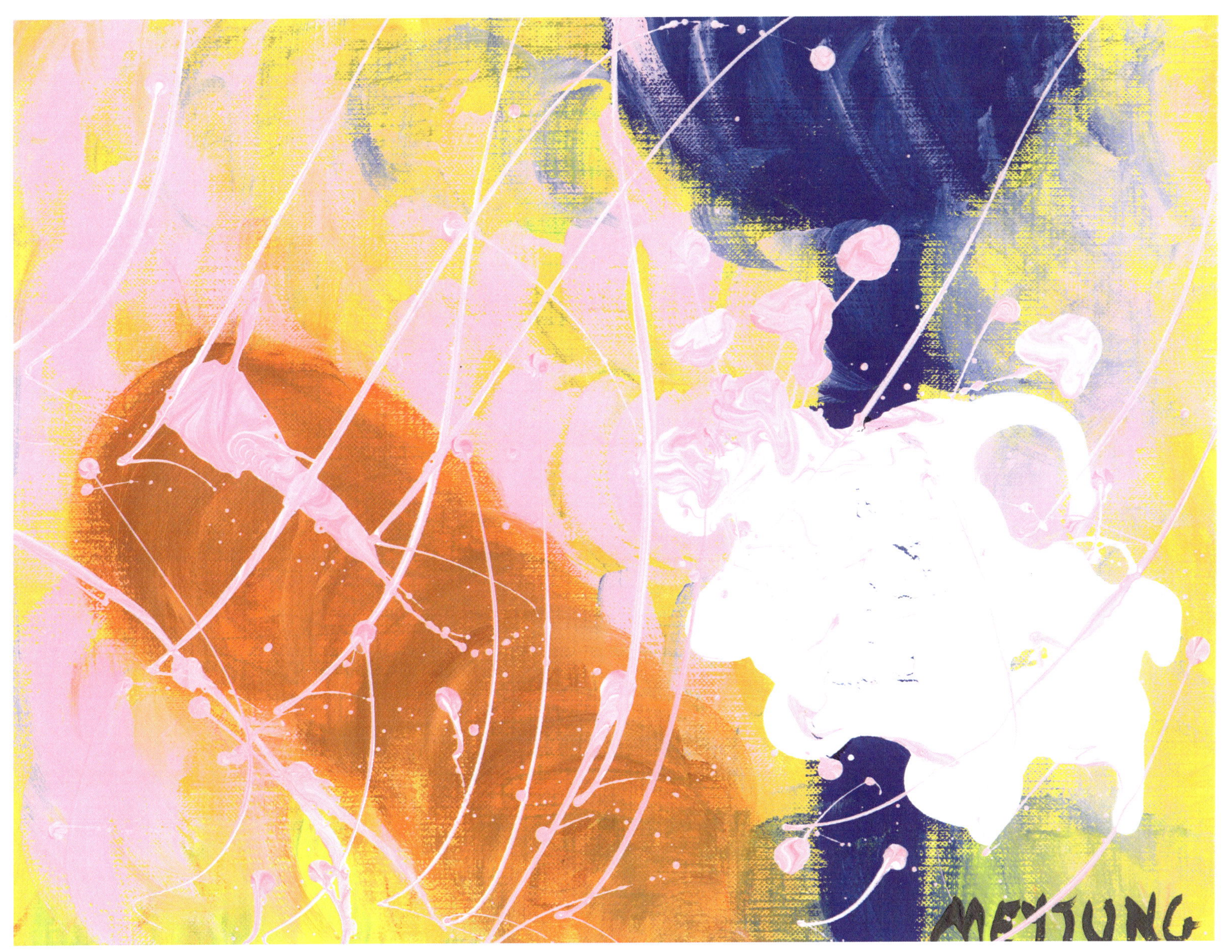

The Whirlwind

NO FEAR (A HAIBUN)

letting go of Self
when the flower's petals fall
the pistil remains
and seeds the new life

das Selbst loslassen
wenn die Blütenblätter fallen
der Stempel bleibt
und sät das neue Leben

MIGRATION

though claimed by many
Tanzania is your home
Mountain of Meru

obwohl von vielen behauptet
Tansania ist dein Zuhause
Berg Meru

EMPTINESS

the moon in the pond
two twenty-two twenty-two
empty illusion

der Mond im Teich
zwei zweiundzwanzig zweiundzwanzig
leere Illusion

MEYLONG TUNGBA

The empty mirror
is stillness watching movement
silence, hearing sound.

Der leere Spiegel
ist Stille, die Bewegung beobachtet
Stille, die Geräusche hört.

PHENOMENA

a waning crescent moon
sweeps across the morning sky
leaving trails of earthshine

eine abnehmende Mondsichel
fegt über den Morgenhimmel
hinterlässt Spuren von Erdschein

AT PLAY

 the trees here are scant
Hope is what shades the children
summer will bring change

die Bäume hier sind knapp
Hoffnung, ist was die Kinder beschattet
der Sommer wird Veränderung bringen

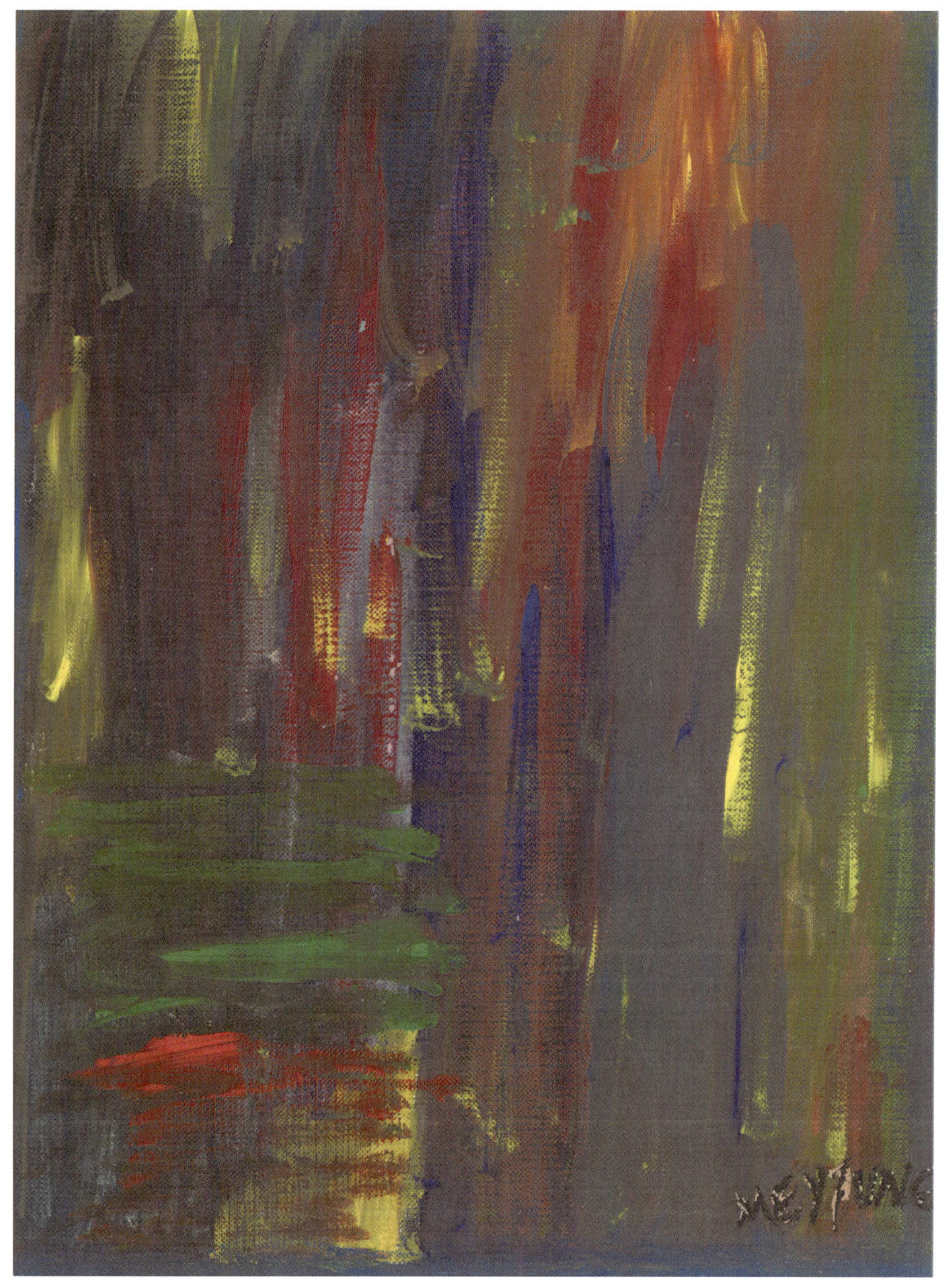

Spiritual (S)elf

FOR CLARISSA

food burning on stove
these haiku won't write themselves
must we always choose?

Essen verbrennt auf dem Herd
diese Haiku schreiben sich nicht
von selbst
müssen wir uns immer
entscheiden?

PURPLE

flitting butterfly
not easily distracted
so often it sees
the color purple

flatternder Schmetterling
nicht leicht ablenkbar
so oft sieht er
die Farbe Lila

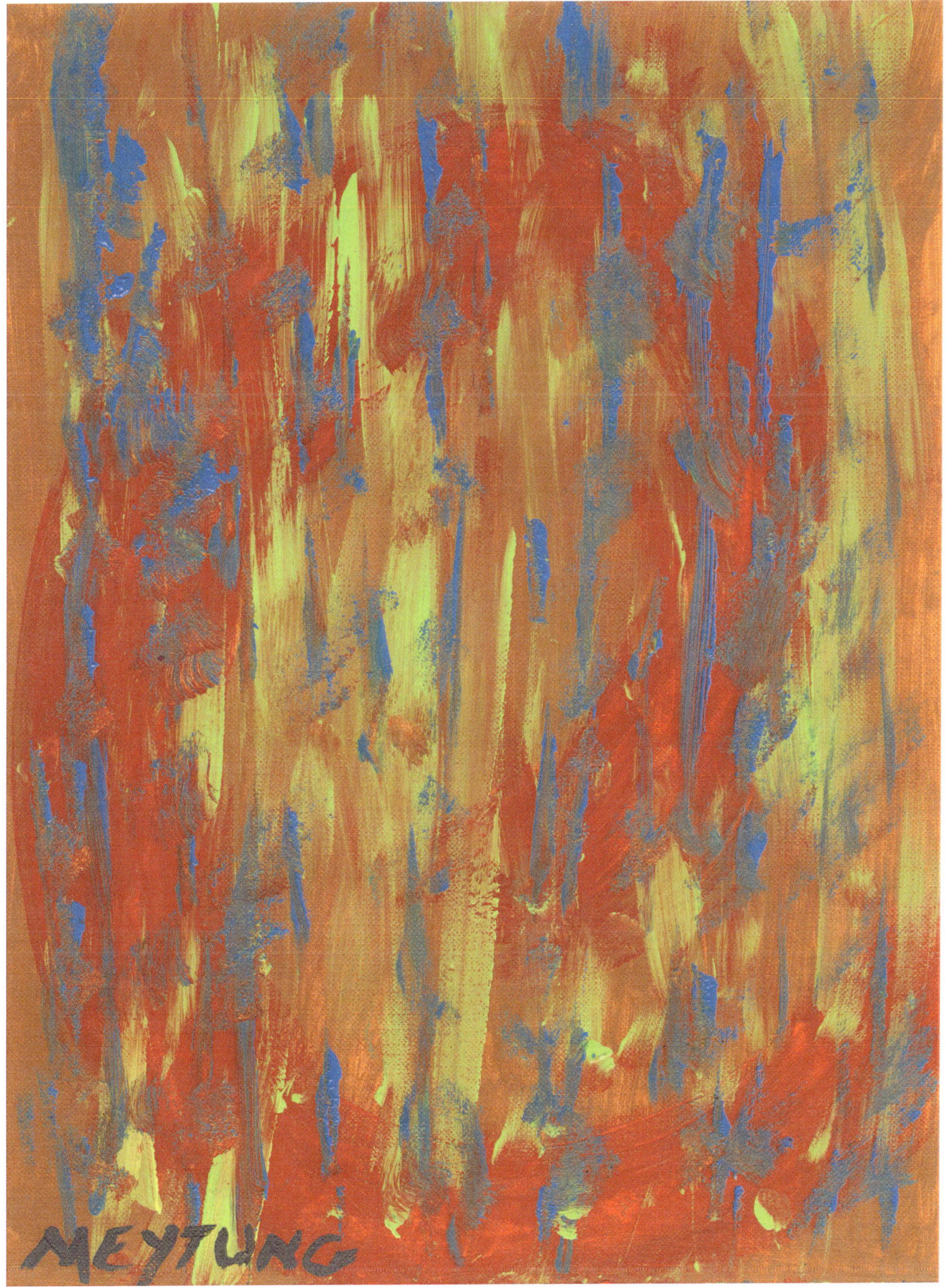

Rebirth

29

(Sketchbook Moments)

SKETCH-
BOOK
MOMENTS

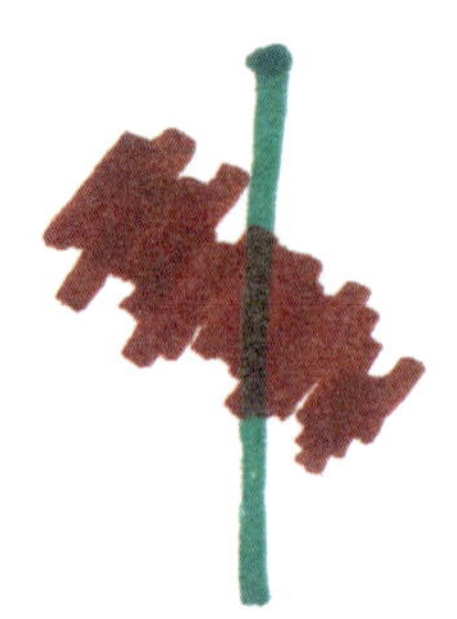

needles pulling threads through air

the texture
of sound

a trash truck beeping

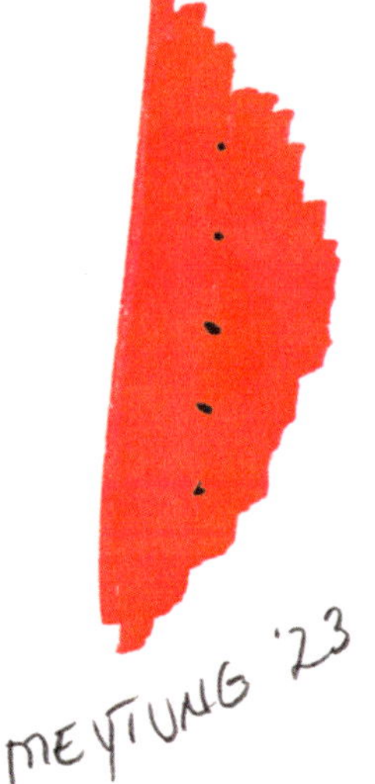

MEYTUNG '23

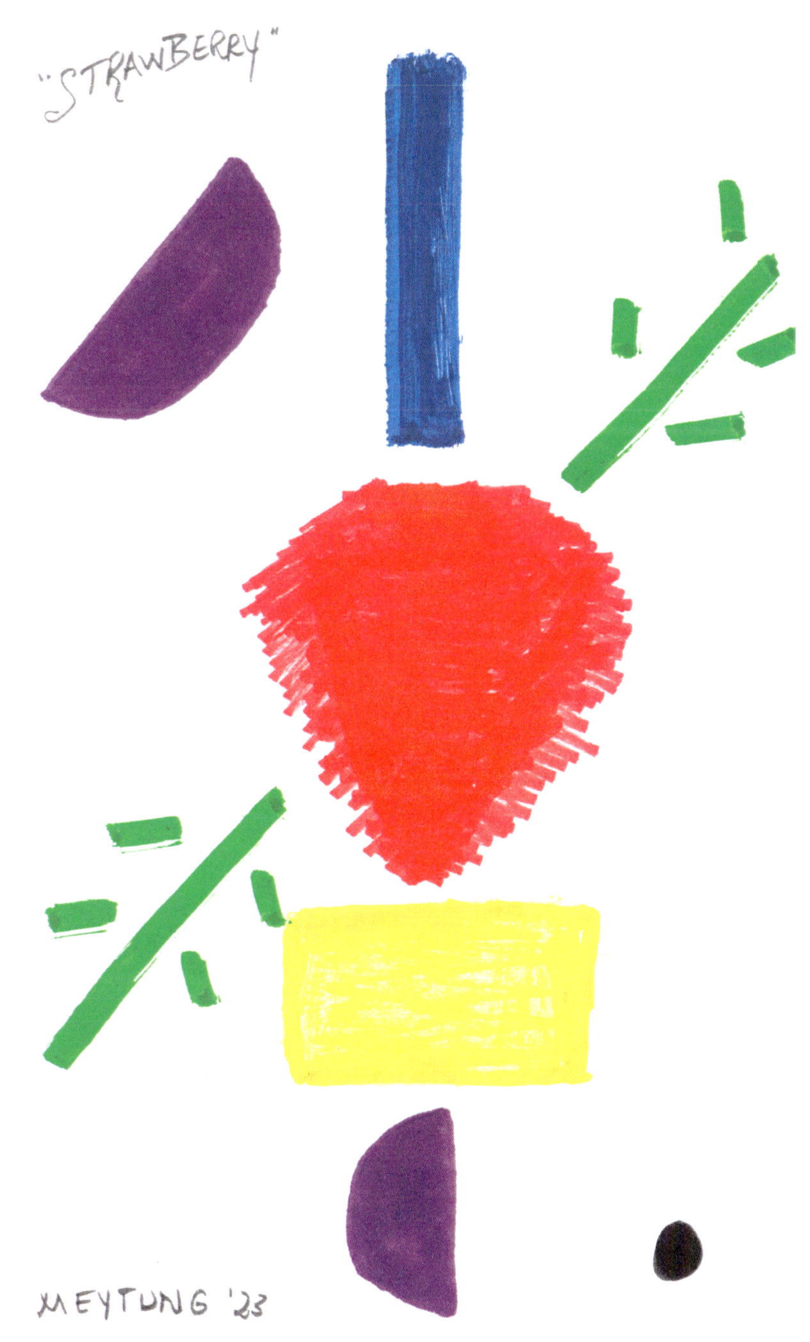

"STRAWBERRY"
MEYTUNG '23

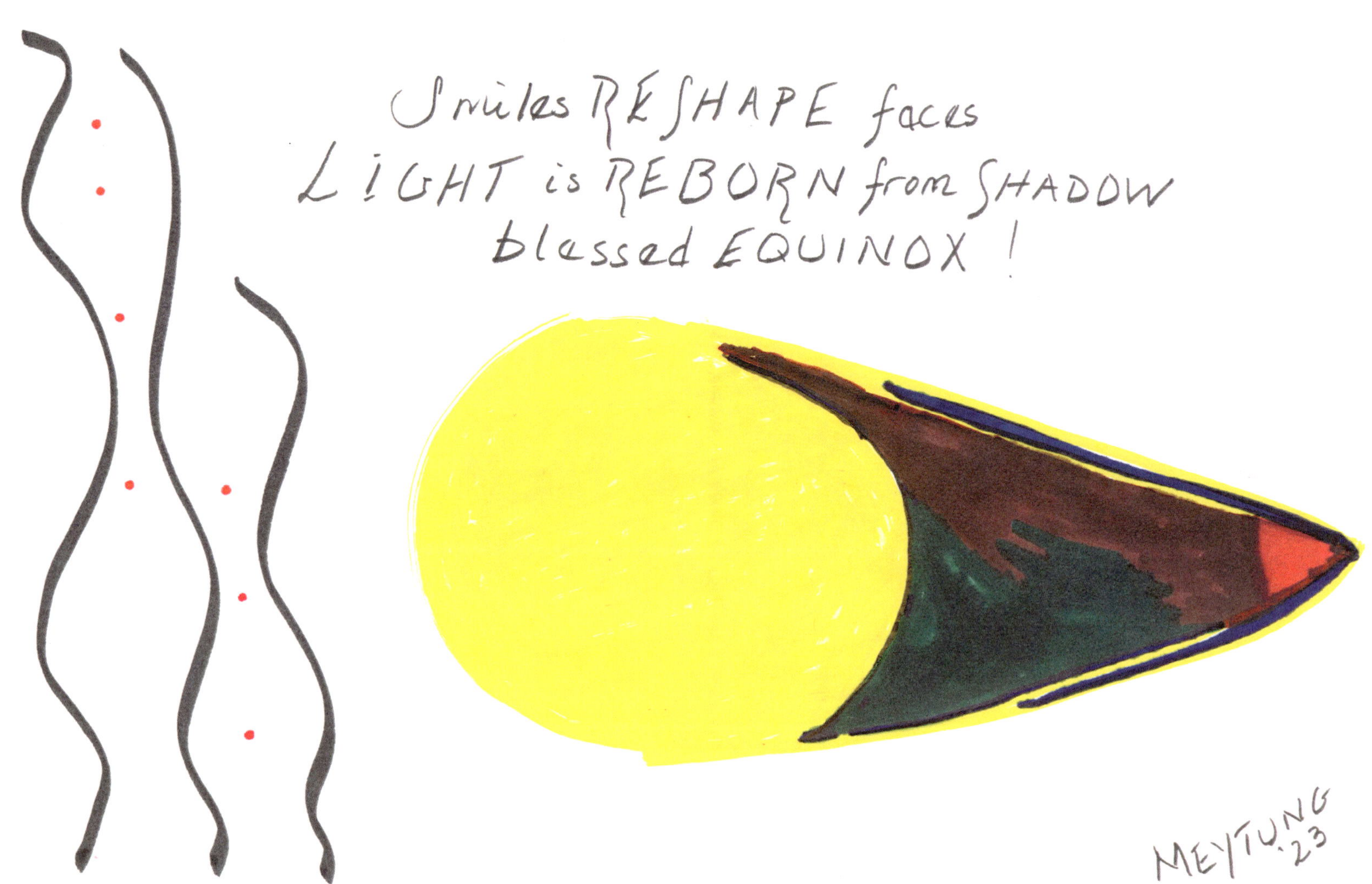
Smiles RESHAPE faces
LIGHT is REBORN from SHADOW
blessed EQUINOX !
MEYTUNG '23

It is said that the Buddha
is defined by three bodies of
enlightenment, the so-called trikaya
of classical Mahayana theory.
These include the dharmakaya, the
body of ultimate reality; the
sambhogakaya, the body of joy;
and the nirmanakaya, the Buddha's
conditioned, human body of
flesh and blood. [Three in One: A Buddhist
Trinity by Reginald
Lion's Bear Ray 9/1/2004]

THE BUDDHA'S THREE BODIES

MEYTUNG
2023

geometric Agnes Martin-
inspired patterns
– when painted use
light water colors +
pastel chalks

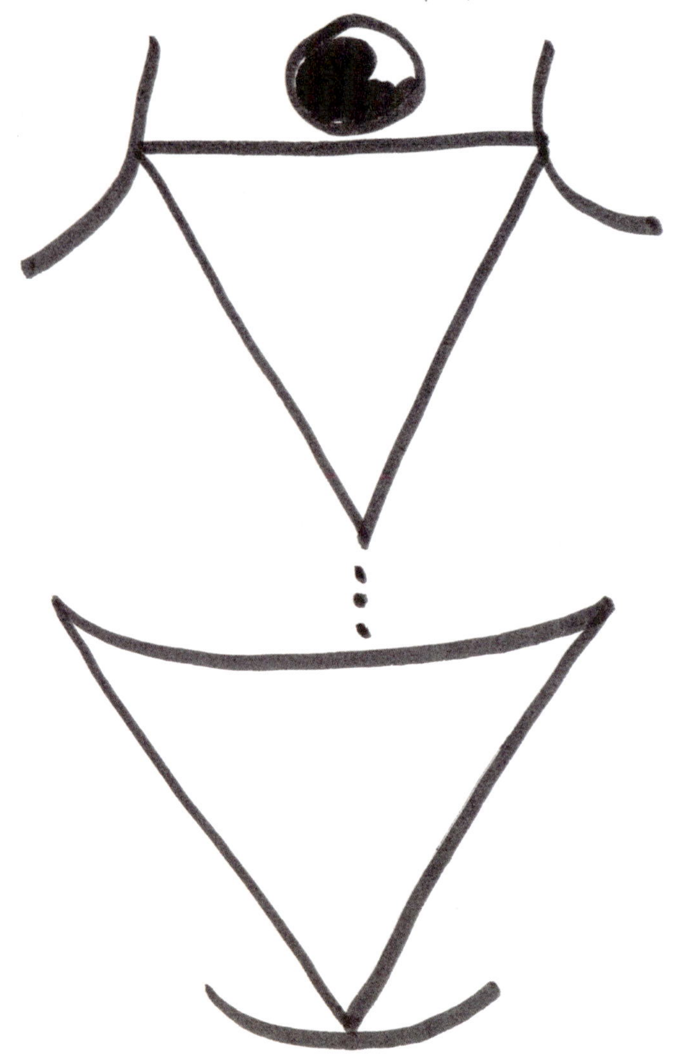

MEYTUNG
'23

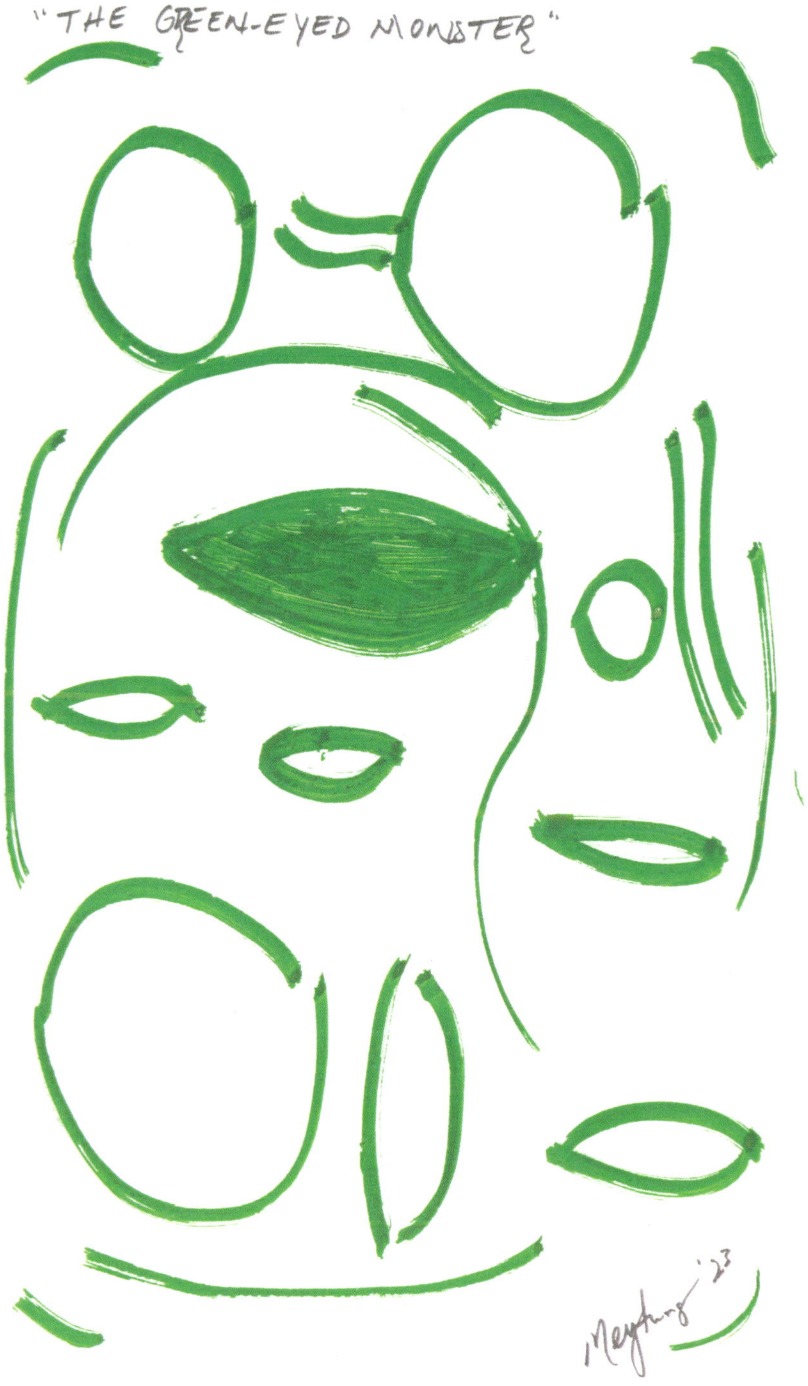

"THE GREEN-EYED MONSTER"

"SOUL"
Meytung '23

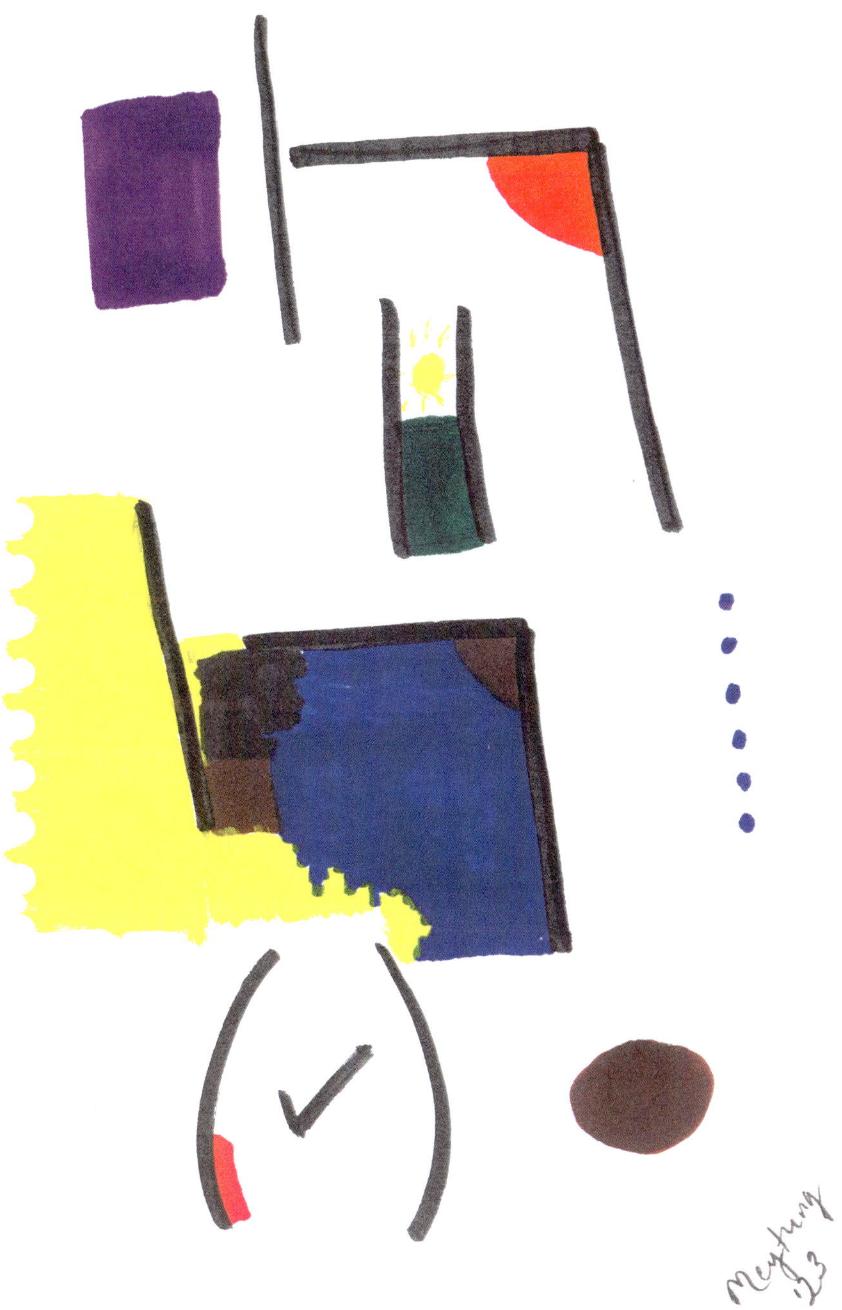

"SHARP -S-"
MEYTUNG '23

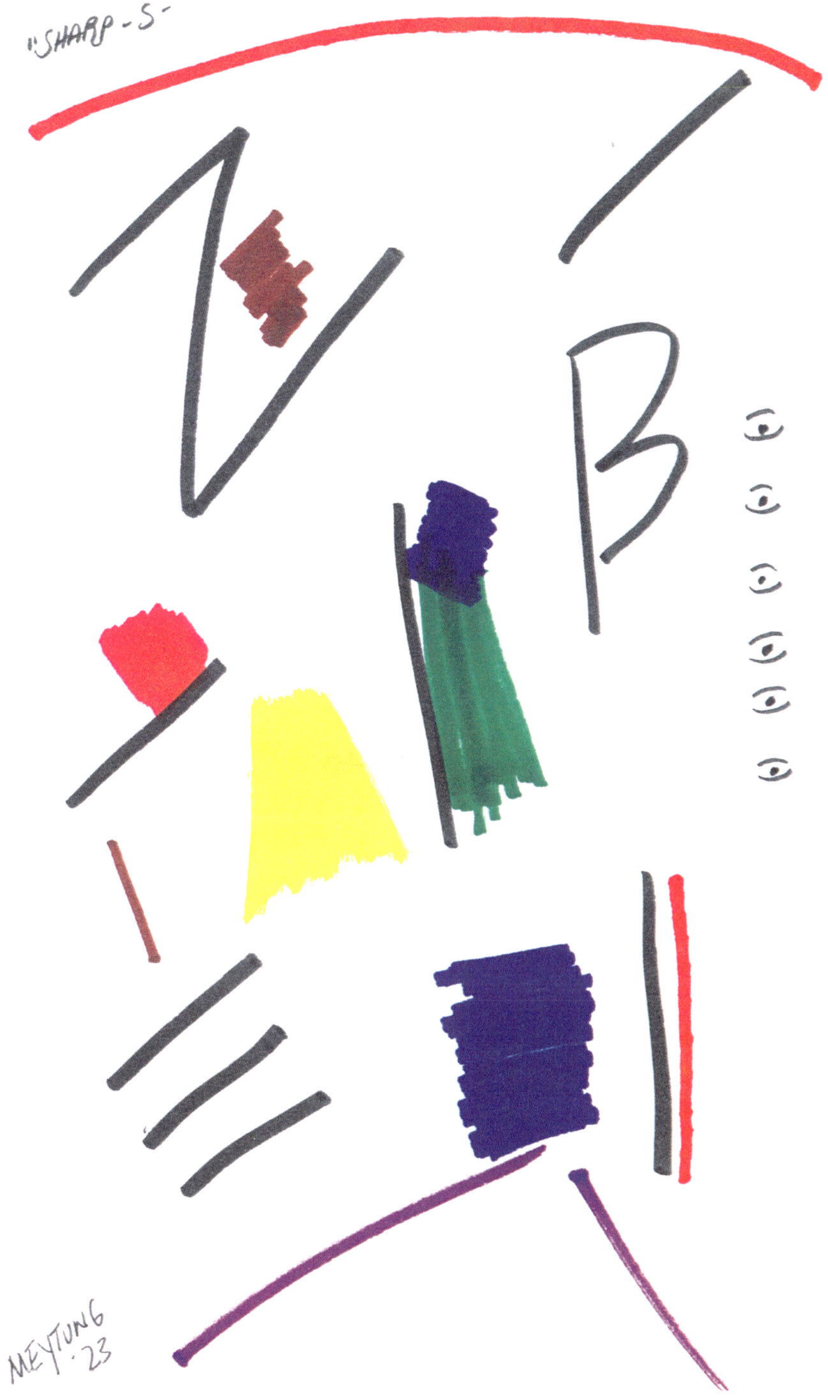

In short, in everything you do,
question how your mind is,
moment by moment.
By being constantly present and
aware
you bring about what helps
others—
this is the practice of a
bodhisattva.

(Tokmé Zongpo, Tibetan scholar / tibetischer Gelehrter, 1291-1371)

Kurz gesagt, bei allem, was du tust,
frage dich, wie es dir geht,
Moment für Moment.
Durch ständige Präsenz und
Bewusstsein
führst du herbei, was anderen
hilft-
das ist die Praxis eines
Bodhisattva.